Compiled by Julia Skinner

With particular reference to the work of Alan Bradley, Clive Hardy,
Matthew Hyde, Dorothy Nicolle, Clare Pye and Jim Rubery

THE FRANCIS FRITH COLLECTION

www.francisfrith.com

First published in the United Kingdom in 2012 by The Francis Frith Collection®

This edition published exclusively for Bradwell Books in 2012
For trade enquiries see: www.bradwellbooks.com or tel: 0800 834 920
ISBN 978-1-84589-687-4

British Library Cataloguing in Publication Data

Did You Know? Cheshire - A Miscellany
Compiled by Julia Skinner
With particular reference to the work of Alan Bradley, Clive Hardy,
Matthew Hyde, Dorothy Nicolle, Clare Pye and Jim Rubery

The Francis Frith Collection
Oakley Business Park,
Wylye Road, Dinton,
Wiltshire SP3 5EU
Tel: +44 (0) 1722 716 376
Email: info@francisfrith.co.uk

www.francisfrith.com

Printed and bound in Malaysia
Contains material sourced from responsibly managed forests

Front Cover: **CHESTER, THE CROSS 1903** 49881p
Frontispiece: **NORTHWICH, THE RIVER WEAVER c1955** N43011
Contents: **CHESTER, THE CATHEDRAL, THE WEST FRONT 1888** 20577

The colour-tinting is for illustrative purposes only, and is not intended to be historically accurate

CONTENTS

INTRODUCTION

Cheshire is a county of delightful contrasts, from the undulating agricultural country of the south of the county with its many black and white timber houses, to the hill country along the edges of the Peaks in the east, from the historic home of the Roman legions at Chester to the industrial heartlands along the Mersey valley. The highest ground lies to the east, where a part of Cheshire is included in the Peak District National Park. This is sheep country, and it is in sharp contrast with the rich farmland of the Cheshire Plain, a landscape of low hills amongst which lie numerous small lakes. This is one of the most important dairy farming areas in the country, and is the home especially of Cheshire Cheese. The north of the county is dominated by the presence of the River Mersey which flows through it, and this area has for a long time been mainly industrial.

One industry has been of major importance to Cheshire since Roman times – the salt industry, based in the centre of the county. However, salt was not the only product being transported around Cheshire and beyond in the past. From the Middle Ages Chester had been a major centre through which wool and cloth were exported. By the 17th century other goods were passing through the county – fragile china from the Potteries, iron products from the new industrial centres of Shropshire and the Black Country, and other raw materials being brought to the manufactories. Many of these goods were moved along rivers, but the rivers were often impassable owing to floods or drought. To begin with, work was done to make them navigable. One of the earliest rivers to be cut in this way was the River Weaver, forming what is now known as the Weaver Navigation. Then, in 1781, the first stretch of the Bridgewater Canal was opened, which revolutionised the transportation of goods, and ushered in the Canal Age. The development of canals, and later the railways, stimulated local industry all over Cheshire throughout the

19th century. With the 20th century, many industrial practices started to change. But the presence of salt under so much of Cheshire was still to play a large part in the county's economy, and new chemical industries were developed both in the heartland of the county around Northwich and Winsford and along the coast at places such as Runcorn and the enormous oil refinery at Stanlow.

In recent memory, the main changes that have taken place in Cheshire have been changes to its borders under the local government reorganisation of 1974. Several new administrative regions were formed which included areas previously in Cheshire – Wirral, Merseyside and Greater Manchester – and Birkenhead, at that time the largest town in Cheshire, was lost to the new region of Wirral. At the same time, districts around Widnes and Warrington, formerly in Lancashire, now became part of Cheshire. But there is much about the county that is still the same, and which gives a strong sense of identity to those who live in the Cheshire of today. This is still a county where both strong rural and industrial traditions sit side by side, and it is perhaps this mix that gives the landscape its beauty and makes the towns and villages so interesting.

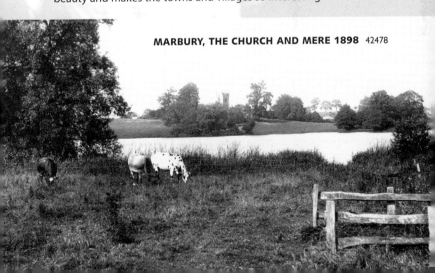

MARBURY, THE CHURCH AND MERE 1898 42478

CHESHIRE DIALECT WORDS AND PHRASES

'Addled' - confused, not thinking straight.

'Chitty' - a young girl.

'Lommeryed' - stupid, simple.

'Mither' - to annoy or bother, thus **'Stop mithering me'** - Stop annoying me.

'Nesh' - cold, or **'neshed'** - feeling cold.

'Spence' - the cupboard under the stairs.

'Me yed's all of a missock' - My head's all in a whirl, I can't think straight.

The name of the Goyt Valley near Macclesfield is derived from the local dialect word **'goyt'** or **'goit'** for 'a stream' or 'a watercourse', originally the Old English word 'gota'.

'There's more than one yew-bow in Chester' - a saying used to console broken-hearted girls spurned by their lovers. It is believed to derive from the days of the Hundred Years' War, when local longbow archers fought at the battles of Crecy, Poitiers and Agincourt.

An old ballad tells how the daughter of a medieval mayor of Chester was betrothed by her father to Lord Luke de Taney, instead of the Welsh knight who she loved. During a ball game with de Taney and some friends near the city wall, she threw the ball over the wall and persuaded de Taney to search for it. While he was gone, she slipped through the tiny Pepper Gate in the wall and escaped with her lover. Her furious father ordered the Pepper Gate to be locked in future, giving rise to the local saying: **'When the daughter is stolen, shut the Pepper Gate'.** Happily, local tradition also says that father and daughter were later reconciled and the Pepper Gate was reopened.

HAUNTED CHESHIRE

The grounds of the former Marbury Hall near Northwich are said to be haunted by a ghostly horse known as the Marbury Dunne, sometimes seen with a lady in the saddle.

The bridge at Farndon which crosses the English-Welsh border marked by the River Dee is reputedly haunted by the spirits of two young Welsh princes, whose murdered bodies were thrown into the river there in medieval times. Their pitiful cries can still be heard…

Chester has many ghost stories. A famous ghost is Sarah, said to haunt her former home at 39 Eastgate Street, now Thornton's chocolate shop. Her lover jilted her on their wedding day, and she hanged herself in despair… The George and Dragon Hotel in Liverpool Road, built on the site of an old Roman cemetery, is reputedly haunted by a Roman legionary on eternal sentry duty – footsteps have been heard pacing along the upper floor late at night, and then coming back, apparently passing through solid brick walls… A ghostly lady is said to look out of an upper window of the old Blue Bell Inn in Northgate Street (now a restaurant), from where she watched her Royalist lover go off to fight at the battle of Rowton Heath during the Civil War; he was killed, but she still waits for him to return… Tudor House in Lower Bridge Street is said to be haunted by the headless ghost of another Royalist soldier killed in the Civil War – during the siege of Chester, a cannonball burst through the building and decapitated him.

Capesthorne Hall at Siddington, Macclesfield, is said to be haunted by a ghostly woman in a grey gown who has been seen many times gliding along corridors in the Hall…

The ghost of Lady Isabella de Boteler reputedly haunts the corridors of Bewsey Old Hall, near Warrington. A modern statue of Lady Isabella stands in the yew maze at the Hall.

The ghostly funeral procession of Sir Piers Legh is said to pass through Lyme Park near Disley; Sir Piers died of battle wounds in 1422, and his tomb is in St Michal's Church in Macclesfield. The weeping ghost of his mistress, Blanche, follows the procession from a distance – she was forbidden to attend the funeral and died of grief soon after his death.

CHESHIRE MISCELLANY

In the Earth's History Gallery of Warrington Museum are some rare footprints of a dinosaur known as chirotherium, which existed in the Warrington area 240 million years ago.

One of the earliest industrial sites in Cheshire was at Tatton Park at Knutsford, where evidence has been found of a Middle Stone Age flint-working site.

The Bridestones at Timbersbrook near Congleton (photograph T219010, below) are the remains of a Neolithic chambered tomb, often described as Cheshire's only megalithic monument. Believed to date back to around 3,000BC, the tomb originally had a covering mound and two other chambers, but all that is left now is the main chamber. The name of the tomb may recall the ancient fertility goddess Bride, but an old legend says the stones are the petrified members of a wedding party, whilst another says a Viking was buried here with his bride, a local Saxon girl.

In the garden of the old rectory in Nether Alderley is a huge scarlet rhododendron, reputedly planted in 1815 to commemorate the Battle of Waterloo and one of the earliest rhododendrons in the county.

**TIMBERSBROOK
THE BRIDESTONES
c1955** T219010

NETHER ALDERLEY, THE VILLAGE SMITHY 1896 37477a

Alderley Edge is one of the most important Bronze Age sites in the country, and the site of the earliest known copper mine in England – a wooden shovel found in the area was carbon dated to 1850-1750 BC. It is now housed in Manchester Museum.

In the Legend of Alderley Edge, a farmer is going over the Edge to market to sell his white mare when an old man stops him and asks to buy the animal. He agrees, and follows the old man to some iron gates which open to reveal a passage into the hill. The farmer follows the old man into a cavern full of a hundred sleeping knights and ninety-nine white mares. The farmer is given as much gold as he wants for his horse and then leaves; the gates clang behind him and he is left alone on the Edge. Never again did he find the iron gates. In the 19th century the local landowners, the Stanleys, landscaped their part of the Edge to fit in with the legend, and fake 'ancient monuments' and the Wizard's Well were built to attract visitors to the area.

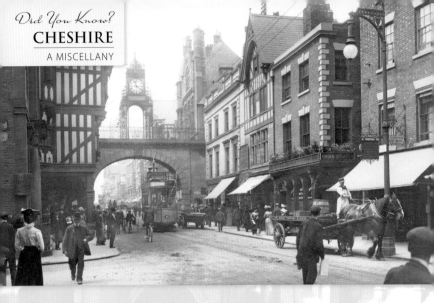

CHESTER, EASTGATE 1903 49887

A grisly reminder of the Iron Age period in Cheshire was found in 1984 when the preserved remains of 'Lindow Man' were found near Wilmslow by workmen cutting peat. He appeared to have been sacrificed by the Celtic people of the area in the 1st century AD. His body, apparently ritually murdered and offered to the gods, was left in the watery peat bog of Lindow Moss. He was possibly sacrificed to try and ward off the Romans, who were invading Cheshire at this time. His remains are now in the British Museum.

The name 'Cheshire' is first recorded in AD980 as 'Legeceasterscir', the 'shire of the city of the legions', a reference to Chester, the headquarters of the Twentieth Legion in Roman times. The Romans built a huge fort there called Deva, which was occupied for over 300 years. The Eastgate in Chester was the entry point of the Roman road, the Via Devana, into Deva; it was rebuilt as an elegant arch in 1769 (photograph 49887, above). Much of modern Chester follows the ground plan of the Roman fort. St Peter's Church, at the top of Bridge Street, sits on the site of its headquarters building (or 'principia').

The Romans settled in the Northwich area around AD70. A variety of industrial processes have been identified from this period of occupation, including several furnaces, smithing hearths, and a potting kiln operated by a person who stamped the name 'Maco' on his wares. So industrious was this part of Cheshire at the time that it has been referred to as the Roman Black Country.

In AD973 the Anglo-Saxon King Edgar, the first 'High King' of England, was rowed along the River Dee at Chester by eight lesser Celtic kings and chieftains as an act of submission to his authority. The park on the south side of the old Dee bridge at Chester is known as Edgar's Field in memory of this event.

In Sandbach's market place are the shafts of two beautiful Saxon crosses (photograph S489701, below). The taller cross is covered with carvings depicting scenes from the life of Christ, and the smaller one is thought to feature scenes from the life of Peada, son of King Penda of Mercia, who was converted to Christianity around AD653.

**SANDBACH
THE MARKET PLACE
2003** S489701

The doorway of the chapel, or oratory, at Prestbury is one of the oldest Norman ecclesiastical examples in Cheshire, and is famous for the zigzag patterns and beaked heads carved on the arch (photograph 37443, below).

Delamere Forest in Cheshire is all that remains of the great forest of Mara that once stretched from the River Mersey to Northwich as a hunting preserve of the Norman kings. 'Delamere' is a French phrase meaning 'of the mere', a reference to the many pools and spongy mosses that are still hidden in the depths of the forest today.

Cheshire has its own Leaning Tower, at the village of Marbury. St Michael's Church was built on sandstone with a mere just below it, and the church has slipped slightly over the years – today its 63ft tower apparently tilts more than two feet out of the vertical. A local legend says that if the ancient yew tree in the churchyard falls, so will the church …

Cheshire churches typically have towers at the west end of the church, rather than over the crossing.

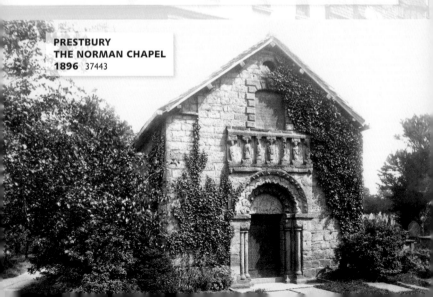

**PRESTBURY
THE NORMAN CHAPEL
1896** 37443

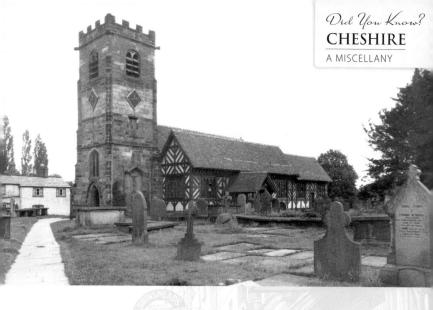

LOWER PEOVER, THE CHURCH c1955 L308011

St Oswald's Church at Lower Peover was founded in 1269 and is notable for its early timberwork – if the timberwork dates from that first church, this could be one of the oldest arcaded wooden frame churches in Europe (photograph L308011, above). Inside the church is a massive chest, hewn from the trunk of a bog oak tree. It used to be a local tradition for a maiden who wished to marry a local farmer to prove her strength and fitness to be his wife by being able to lift the heavy lid of the chest with one arm.

One of the oldest houses in Weaverham, west of Northwich, is Poplar Cottage on Northwich Road, which dates from the 1600s. The cottage used to have a small room on the ground floor that was slightly lower than the rest of the building and was traditionally used as a 'birthing chamber'. After its birth in the ground floor room the newborn child would then be carried up the step, to fulfil an old saying that in order to do well for yourself in later life you had to take 'one step up' after birth – hence the expression 'going up in the world'.

A stained glass window in All Saints' Church at Daresbury depicts characters from the stories of Alice in Wonderland. Charles Lutwidge Dodgeson, better known as the author Lewis Carroll, was baptised in the church in 1832. His father was the vicar here, and Dodgeson was born in the vicarage, since burnt down. Many characters featured in Lewis Carroll's books are thought to have been inspired by the strange carvings in the church.

The Cheshire Cat immortalised by Lewis Carroll in 'Alice's Adventures in Wonderland' is traditionally associated with the county, but no one really knows where the story of the grinning cat came from. It may have originated from a carving of a cat on a corbel of the tower of St Wilfrid's Church at Grappenhall, possibly put there as a 'signature' of a man called Catterall who worked on the church; or perhaps it came from the custom of making early Cheshire cheeses in an oval shape, which resembled a curled-up cat. But the Cheshire Cat may not even be a cat at all – the story may derive from the arms of Hugh, the first Earl of Chester, nicknamed 'Lupus', or 'the Wolf', because of his ferocity; his coat of arms depicted the snarling face of a wolf, which may have been sardonically referred to as a grinning cat.

The ruined Beeston Castle near Tarporley is famous for the treasure that was supposedly hidden here by Richard II in 1399 on his way to Ireland. On his return he was captured by the forces of the future Henry IV, and met his death in Pontefract Castle soon afterwards. Searches have been made, but nothing has ever been found!

The village of Gawsworth between Macclesfield and Congleton is notable for its timber-framed Old Hall, once the home of Mary Fitton, a maid of honour to Elizabeth I and one of the contenders as the mysterious Dark Lady of Shakespeare's sonnets. A famous 18th-century occupant of the Old Hall was Samuel 'Maggoty' Johnson, an eccentric fiddle-player and playwright who was also the last professional jester in England. He died in 1773 and was buried at his request in Maggoty's Wood on the outskirts of the village.

Thought to be the oldest inhabited secular building in Cheshire, Chorley Hall near Alderley Edge was started in the 14th century, when moated manor houses were at the height of fashion – seen in photograph 37470, below. The half-timbered wing was added in the 16th century.

ALDERLEY EDGE, CHORLEY HALL 1896 37470

13

Wilmslow was combined from four older townships of Chorley, Fulshaw, Pownall Fee and Bollin Fee – the latter is commemorated in the name of the Bollin Fee pub in Swan Street. 'Wilmslow' was originally just the name for the mound where the town's parish church of St Bartholomew stands, and only became the name for the whole town in 1894, when the four townships were combined into one new civil parish. St Bartholomew's Church has medieval origins but was greatly 'restored' in the 19th century. In the floor of the chancel is the oldest memorial brass in Cheshire, dated 1460, which commemorates Sir Robert Booth ('del Bothe') and his lady Dulcia (or 'Douce'). Holding hands, Sir Robert is depicted on the memorial brass in plate armour with a greyhound at his feet, and Dulcia has a smaller dog at hers.

In the 18th century the Wilmslow area was best known for its cottage industry making silk buttons, although cotton was also produced there. However, it became a thriving commuter community after the railways came in 1842, popular with Stockport and Manchester-based business people wishing to live in more rural surroundings.

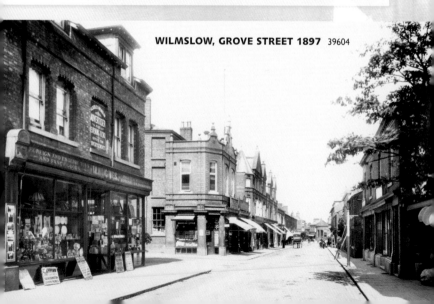

WILMSLOW, GROVE STREET 1897 39604

KNUTSFORD, ROYAL GEORGE HOTEL, KING STREET c1955 K47017

South-west of Wilmslow is Knutsford, reputedly named after King Canute (1016-1035), who forded the River Lily there. In the background of photograph K47018 (above) is the landmark building on King Street that was originally built in 1907 to house Knutsford's Urban District Council; its distinctive tower is a memorial to the 19th-century author Mrs Elizabeth Gaskell (1810-1865), who came to the town as a young child after her mother's death and was brought up there by her aunt. She taught at the local Unitarian chapel Sunday School, and she and her husband William are buried in the chapel yard. After her marriage Mrs Gaskell and her husband lived in Manchester, where Mr Gaskell was a Unitarian minister. What she saw there inspired her to write several novels sympathetically depicting the hardship of life in 19th-century industrial England, including 'Ruth', 'Mary Barton', and 'North and South'. However, Mrs Gaskell is probably best known for 'Cranford', first published in 1851, which was dramatised in 2007 as a television serial by the BBC; the book gives a wonderfully evocative picture of life in a small country town in the mid 1800s, for which Knutsford is believed to have been the inspiration.

15

CHESTER, THE CROSS 1903 49881

Chester's proximity to Wales often led to friction between its citizens and Welshmen in medieval times. Henry IV banned Welshmen from the streets of Chester after sunset and forbade them from carrying any weapons other than a knife for their meat.

Chester was the most important port in northern England in the Middle Ages, through which wool and cloth were exported. Then disaster struck, as the River Dee silted up. Eventually a small hamlet called Liverpool took over as the major port for the area.

The corner of Eastgate Street and Bridge Street in Chester is known as The Cross (photograph 49881, above). A medieval cross stood here until it was demolished during the Civil War, but it was restored and re-erected on its original site in 1975. The Cross is where Chester's famous medieval Mystery Plays were performed, a series of dramatic stories drawn from the Bible that were enacted by medieval craftsmen and guildsmen in the 14th century. Chester's Mystery Plays were revived in 1951 and are performed every five years, a valued part of the city's cultural heritage.

Photograph 49881 (opposite) of The Cross in Chester shows the Rows for which the city is so famous. The Rows consist of continuous galleries above the ground-floor level giving access to other, totally separate, shops. They probably started to develop in the form that we see them today as early as the 13th century.

Chester is sometimes called 'The Walled City' as its medieval walls form the most complete circuit (two miles long) of medieval walls around any town or city in England.

During the Civil War, Chester was loyal to King Charles I. On 24th September 1645 the battle of Rowton Heath was fought just outside the city, as King Charles watched from the city walls. The Royalist forces were defeated and King Charles fled to Wales, leaving Chester to be besieged by Parliamentarian forces; the citizens held out for five months, reduced to eating rats and dogs, until starvation forced them to surrender.

A famous Chester building is God's Providence House in Watergate Street, the front of which bears the carved inscription 'God's Providence is mine inheritance'. This is said to commemorate the household's escape from death during an outbreak of plague in the 17th century.

In the south-east corner of Chester's city walls are six flights of stone stairs known as the Wishing Steps. Local legend says your wish will be fulfilled if you can run to the top, back to the bottom, and then up again without drawing breath. A similar tradition is linked with the 108 Steps in Macclesfield, where you will gain your heart's desire if you can run up the steps in one breath.

18th-century Macclesfield was such a centre of the British silk industry that it was nicknamed 'Silk Town'. Mill Street is where Charles Roe established a mill in 1743 for 'throwing' silk (making silk thread from silkworm cocoons)., Other mills in the town soon followed, silk weaving was introduced c1790, and by 1817 Macclesfield had twelve manufacturers of woven silk material. The town showcases its industrial past in a variety of museums, from Paradise Mill in Park Lane (with weaving demonstrations on old machinery) to exhibits made from silk in the costume collection at the town's Heritage Centre, housed in the former Big Sunday School building (see opposite page).

Macclesfield's other nickname is 'Treacle Town'. Local tradition says this derives from an incident when a merchant spilt a quantity of treacle on Hibel Road, which the townspeople were quick to salvage, although another explanation is that it dates from when some mill-owners in the town provided barrels of treacle to unemployed weavers.

Photograph 40442 (below) shows the cast iron fountain which used to be the centrepiece of Macclesfield's Park Green, but which went for scrap during the Second World War. Apparently its twin still exists in the Scottish town of Strathpeffer.

MACCLESFIELD, PARK GREEN 1897 40442

MACCLESFIELD, THE SUNDAY SCHOOL 1897 40460

Sunday schools were where most children in the past received a rudimentary education, until the passing of the Education Act in 1870. In 1796 John Whitaker started a non-denominational school in Macclesfield in premises in Pickford Street. The scheme was popular, and by 1812, with more than 2,000 children attending various Sunday schools around the town each week, Whitaker needed one large building to house them all. A fine model of the proposed building was made, which still exists, which was probably trundled round the town on a barrow to raise funds. Thanks to donations, the Big Sunday School, as it was known, opened in 1814 (see photograph 40460, above). The first Superintendent of the new Sunday School was John Whitaker himself, who started the school 'to lessen the sum of human wretchedness'. There is a monument to John Whitaker outside the Sunday School building, which now houses Macclefield Heritage Centre.

On the staircase of Macclesfield's Town Hall is a statue of Artemis, goddess of the moon, by Hamo Thorneycroft, one of the most famous sculptors of the Victorian age.

MACCLESFIELD, THE PARISH CHURCH OF ST MICHAEL AND ALL ANGELS 1903 49456

The parish church of St Michael and All Angels in Macclesfield has two towers, unusual for a parish church (see photograph 49456, above). The big one is the bell tower, and the smaller tower is actually a house attached to the Savage chapel (built 1505), which holds a fine series of 15th-century carved alabaster effigies. The monument to Thomas, Earl Rivers of Rock Savage (d.1695) is especially noteworthy but also of interest is the tomb of the 8th John Savage and his first wife, dated 1597 – John's wife, Elizabeth Manners, daughter of the Earl of Rutland, lies higher than her husband because of her more noble birth.

The English surname Maxfield is derived from the place-name of Macclesfield. In medieval times, a local name was often either assumed by an individual from the patrimonial estate if he held land, or was used to describe someone's place of residence or birth. Thus the surname Maxfield described someone who came from Macclesfield.

The Macclesfield Canal was the last canal to be built in England, opening in 1831. It was built to transport cotton and silk as well as coal and stone; today, used mainly by holiday-makers, it is considered one of the prettiest waterways in the country.

Macclesfield was the birthplace of Hovis bread, made from a flour especially rich in wheatgerm; the brand was developed by S Fitton & Sons Ltd, whose mill operated on the banks of the Macclesfield Canal. The name 'Hovis' was invented by a London student, Herbert Grimes, who was inspired by the Latin phrase 'hominis vis' ('the strength of man'), after Fittons set a national competition to find a trading name for the bread made from their patented flour. The former Hovis warehouse by the canal is now apartments.

Bollington is a few miles north of Macclesfield. 'A thriving village with some collieries and extensive cotton factories' was how the town was described in 1848. Those factories were especially renowned for the quality of their Liberty cottons. This view looks down on the town from an aqueduct along the Macclesfield Canal.

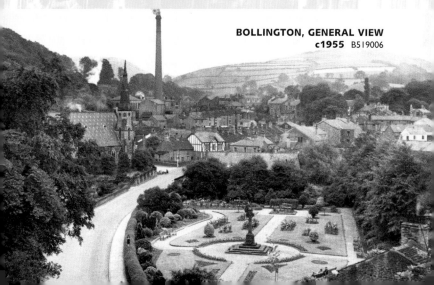

BOLLINGTON, GENERAL VIEW
c1955 B519006

Macclesfield is known as 'Silk Town', but Congleton actually produced the most silk of the two towns. A water-powered silk throwing mill was built beside the River Dane in the 1750s (photograph 48675, below), only the fourth such mill in the country, and at that time the largest. Its machinery was driven by a single waterwheel, later supplemented by one of the first steam engines in Cheshire. The original silk mill became known as 'Old Mill' as others were built around the town, and Congleton became an early industrial centre. The Old Mill was demolished in 2002.

Congleton's silk industry declined in the 19th century, causing great unemployment in the town. This led to the introduction of the trade of 'fustian cutting', in which the looped pile of a material like corduroy was slit with a knife to produce a velvet-like fabric. The worker had to walk the entire length of the mill, slitting one row of loops in a stretched-out piece of material with a special knife, and then walk back again, slitting the next row. A worker could walk over 20 miles on a shift, and bending over the work led to a permanent stoop.

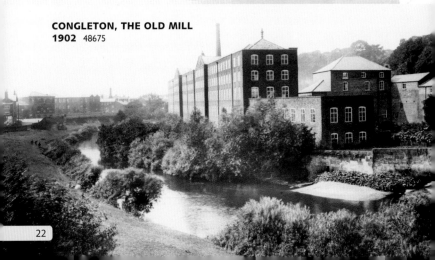

CONGLETON, THE OLD MILL
1902 48675

CONGLETON, LAWTON STREET 1898 42154

Cruel contraptions known as scold's bridles or branks were used in the 16th and 17th centuries to punish nagging wives, and to silence women spreading gossip, slander or religious sedition, or disturbing the peace with rowdy behaviour. They usually consisted of a metal cage fitted around the head, with a metal bar holding down the tongue. There are several examples in Cheshire museums: in West Park Museum in Macclesfield, in Warrington Museum, and in Congleton Museum. Congleton's scold's bridle is a collar and chain which was also used by the townsmen in the past to tether nagging wives to a wall in the market place. It was last used in 1824, when Jane Runcorn was sentenced to wear it whilst being led through the town as punishment for shouting abuse at local churchwardens who had ordered the town's pubs to be closed during a church service.

It is an old tradition for Congleton people to climb their local 'mountain', The Cloud, for a dawn service on Easter Day.

Little Moreton Hall is an outstanding moated timber-framed house near Congleton (photograph 48670, below), parts of which date from the 16th century. Its crowning glory is the long gallery above the gatehouse. As with many old houses, there is a secret room; the difference at Little Moreton is that a second secret room exists – beneath the moat.

The boundary between Cheshire and Staffordshire runs along the top of a ridge to the south of Congleton, topped at a prominent point by another fascinating building, Mow Cop Castle (see photograph 42173, opposite). This sham castle is in fact a folly, built in the 1750s to improve the view from Rode Hall. Mow Cop holds a prominent place in the history of the Primitive Methodist movement, being the site of some of its early meetings.

CONGLETON, LITTLE MORETON HALL 1902 48670

CONGLETON, MOW COP CASTLE 1898 42173

Nine villages in central Cheshire compete every summer in the old art of gooseberry showing. The gooseberries are weighed in the ancient measures of pennyweights and grains, and the growers compete in classes for the heaviest berry, twins, triplets and colours. For 16 years (until the record was beaten in 2009) the record for the largest gooseberry ever grown was held by Kelvin Archer for a Montrose Berry exhibited at the Marton Village Show in Congleton in 1993, which weighed 39 pennyweights and 9 grains (61.9g – just over 2oz).

It is said that the people of Barnton, near Northwich, in central Cheshire were once so poor that they could only afford to eat 'jam butties' – so the town came to be known as 'Jam Town'.

LYMM, THE BRIDGEWATER CANAL c1960 L122053

In 1759, the Duke of Bridgewater financed the building of the first
proper canal – the Bridgewater Canal – to transport coal from
his mine at Worsley to the industrial areas of Manchester. When
the first stretch of this canal opened in 1781 it revolutionised the
transportation of goods, and ushered in a frenzy of canal building
all around the country. After the Second World War, the use of canals
around England for the transportation of industrial goods almost
completely ended. However, the boat seen on the Bridgewater Canal
at Lymm in photograph L122053 (above) is still working in the 1960s,
carrying a cargo of coal.

Quarry Bank Cotton Mill at Styal stands on the banks of the River Bollin near Wilmslow in east Cheshire. One of the best preserved textile mills of the Industrial Revolution, it is now a museum of the cotton industry in the care of the National Trust. It was originally water-powered, although the waterwheel is long gone. The mill is a rare survivor from the early stages of the Industrial Revolution, when the new water-powered mills were sited by fast-flowing streams to power their machinery. Consequently these mills were often in isolated areas, and the owners had to create a complete infrastructure to support their industry, building housing for the mill workers within walking distance of work, as well as shops and places of worship. All this can be seen at Styal. Between Quarry Bank Mill and the village of Styal itself was the Apprentice House, where pauper children were housed, receiving their keep and training in return for working in the mill. Quarry Bank Mill now welcomes many visitors, especially school children who come to experience what it was like to be a child worker and to see the mill still producing cotton cloth by water power.

STYAL, THE COTTON MILL 1897 39616

27

CREWE, QUEEN'S PARK, THE MAIN ENTRANCE c1950 C316002

Crewe was just a small hamlet until a number of railways came there in the 19th century, making it a major railway intersection. Crewe now has one of the busiest railway stations in the country. The town's growth was also due to the locomotive production works founded there by the Grand Junction Railway Company in 1843. By the end of the 19th century there were over 40,000 people living in Crewe, nearly a quarter of whom were linked in some way with the railway industry. In 1887, the year of Queen Victoria's golden jubilee, the London North Western Railway Company presented Queen's Park to the town, a gift that also commemorated 50 years of the railway in Crewe. Photograph C316002 (above) shows the clock tower near the main entrance to Queen's Park. It was built using subscriptions from workers in all departments of the LNWRC 'as a token of their appreciation of the generosity of their Board of Directors (who) presented the park to the town'. It is decorated with a carved head on each side, depicting three board members and Queen Victoria.

By the 1930s the number of men required in Crewe's railway industry was in decline, as railways faced competition from motor-cars and aeroplanes. Fortunately, Crewe's skilled workforce was what the new aero engine industry required, and in 1938 Rolls-Royce set up production there. Throughout the Second World War the company produced engines for Spitfires, Hurricanes, Lancasters and Mosquitoes, making it a prime target for enemy air raids – on one occasion a direct hit on the Rolls-Royce works killed 16 workers. After the war, production was changed to Rolls-Royce cars, and the Crewe factory became particularly famous; for a time road signs in the vicinity all advertised 'Crewe and Nantwich – Home of the Best Cars in the World'. Despite this association with cars, it is said that Crewe has the highest number of cyclists for a town of its size in all of Britain!

Listed in the 'Domesday Book' of 1086 as 'Eleacir', the name of the town of Alsager, east of Crewe, tells us that the area of the town was once 'Aelle's field or ploughed land'.

CREWE, MARKET STREET AND THE SQUARE c1955   C316030

Cheshire's saltfields were laid down around 200 million years ago, when a tropical sea covered the area. Salt has always been a valuable commodity, both as a food preservative and in chemical and manufacturing industries. The salt pits at Nantwich were probably first worked by the Romans. In 1583 Nantwich was devastated by a great fire. Queen Elizabeth I donated money to help rebuild the town and encouraged a nationwide fund-raising appeal, showing the importance of Nantwich and its salt industry to the country's economy. Number 41 High Street, known as the 'Queen's Aid House', was built the year after the fire (the building with the spike on the gable end on the right of the photograph below), and bears an inscription commemorating the queen's help in rebuilding the town:

God grant out ryal Queen
In England long to raign
For she hath put her helping
Hand to bild this town again.

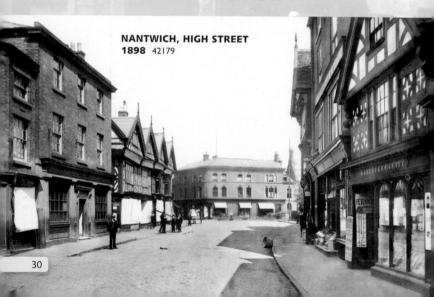

NANTWICH, HIGH STREET
1898 42179

30

NANTWICH, CHURCHES MANSION 1898 42184

Another of Nantwich's historic buildings is Churches Mansion in Hospital Street (photograph 42184, above), which was built in 1577 for a wealthy salt merchant named Rychard Churche. The corbels on the exterior of the house are decorated with carved figures and symbols, including a salamander, a small lizard believed to be immune to fire probably placed there as a charm to protect the house from burning down; it worked, as this building was one of the few structures to survive the fire that destroyed Nantwich in 1583.

Barker Street in Nantwich recalls the leather-tanning industry that used to be important to the town; the bark from oak trees was used in the tanning process. Shoemaking was also once an important local industry – by 1880, over 400,000 pairs of shoes and boots were being produced in Nantwich every year.

Welsh Row in Nantwich was so named because this street leads westwards from the town towards Wales. In medieval times it was called 'le Frog Row', which was apparently a reference to the open sewer that then ran down the centre of the street.

**NANTWICH, THE PARISH CHURCH FROM THE SOUTH EAST
1898** 42189

Nantwich's beautiful church is known as 'the cathedral of south
Cheshire', shown in photograph 42189, above. This view shows the
fine octagonal crossing tower enclosing the old belfry. One of the
glories of the church is the wonderful carving detail in the choir,
especially the choir canopies, but the misericords in the church
are especially delightful, featuring carvings of exotic animals,
a mermaid, and even a comic carving of a woman beating her
husband with a ladle. On the north side of the outside wall of the
church, by a waterspout, is a small sculpture of the devil catching
a woman with her hand in a pitcher. Apparently, men working on
the church in medieval times returned home to their lodgings to
find their landlady stealing money they had hidden in a pitcher for
safekeeping. They got their revenge by immortalising her dishonesty
in stone.

Dorfold Hall at Nantwich was built for Ralph Wilbraham between 1616 and 1621 (photograph 42194, below) and is one of the best houses of its period in Cheshire. The Great Chamber is particularly fine with its panelling and stunning plaster ceiling, covered with fleur-de-lis, thistles and roses, symbols of the royal houses of England and Scotland.

Cheshire's other historic old salt towns are Middlewich and Northwich. Amongst other meanings, 'wich' or 'wych' in a place-name is a reference to a salt-producing town. The name of Middlewich means it is the middle town between Northwich and Nantwich.

The church of St Michael and All Angels in Middlewich has a carved wooden screen in its Venables chapel depicting the Venables family crest of a dragon with a baby in its jaws. Legend says this commemorates Thomas Venables, who in the Middle Ages fought a ferocious dragon that lived in a pool at Moston, near Middlewich. Thomas shot the dragon in the eye with an arrow just as it was about to devour a child, and then slew it. The legend is remembered in the name of Dragon's Lane, which runs between the A530 Nantwich-Middlewich Road, and the A533 Sandbach-Middlewich Road.

NANTWICH, DORFOLD HALL 1898 42194

Like Nantwich and Middlewich, Northwich is a town that has literally, as well as metaphorically, been built upon salt. In 1670, workmen prospecting for coal happened upon rock salt, a discovery that rocketed Northwich to the forefront of salt production. After 1779, new borings revealed even deeper and more extensive salt beds, up to 12ft thick and of exceptional quality, and salt production from 23 local salt mines increased dramatically to over 100,000 tons per year by the end of the 18th century. The in-depth history of salt production in Northwich is told at the excellent Weaver Hall Museum and Workhouse on London Road in the town.

An unfortunate side effect of Cheshire's salt mining industry was serious subsidence throughout the saltfield. Cavernous holes appeared in streets, cracks developed in roads and walls, buildings tilted at crazy angles and others sank below ground, or collapsed. For many years the salt companies refused to accept liability for subsidence and the damage it was causing, but in 1891 the Brine Pumping (Compensation of Subsidence) Act was passed, and people could claim compensation.

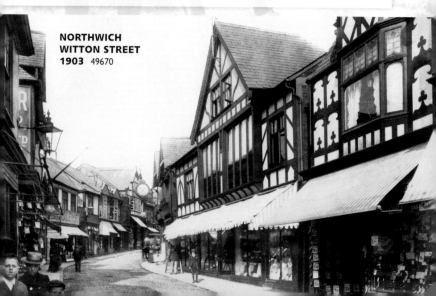

**NORTHWICH
WITTON STREET
1903** 49670

NORTHWICH, THE SWING BRIDGE 1900 45422x

Photograph 45422x (above) shows Town Bridge over the River Weaver at Northwich a year after it was constructed in 1899 (the man in the peaked cap on the left was the bridge's operator). Town Bridge and Hayhurst Bridge (built in 1898) in Northwich were the first electrically powered swing bridges in Britain, and the first to be built on floating pontoons; they can be swung open in order to let vessels pass along the river. Both initiatives came about because of subsidence due to salt extraction; electric cables, unlike pipes, bend rather than break when the ground gives way, and a floating pivot is totally unaffected by subsidence.

NORTHWICH, THE RIVER WEAVER c1960 N43019

The River Weaver has been used to move salt away from Cheshire for centuries, but originally only along its lower tidal reaches. Salt was brought to the river on packhorses to meet the oncoming tide, and sailing barges would load at high water and depart for Liverpool and other ports on the ebbing tide. In the 18th century the river was canalised from Frodsham through Northwich to Winsford, 20 miles inland. The Weaver Navigation was completed by 1732, with the course of the river straightened out, the channel deepened and a series of locks built that could accommodate cargo boats of 100 tons. Northwich became an inland port.

The town of Winsford did not exist until the River Weaver was canalised, linking local salt fields with the River Mersey. Winsford sits on beds of rock salt laid down about 200 million years ago. Salt mining has been carried out there for centuries, and salt is still extracted locally from the only remaining working rock salt mine in Britain. Cheshire's salt mines are enormous, so large that miles of subterranean road systems, big enough for double-decker buses, have been formed below ground to travel on.

At Anderton, near Northwich, the Trent & Mersey Canal and the River Weaver ran parallel with each other, with the canal being just 50 feet above the river. The innovative Anderton Boat Lift, 'the wonder of the waterways', linked the Trent & Mersey Canal (above) with the River Weaver (below). Narrow boats entered a caisson along the trough to the left and were lowered down to the river – one such can be seen sandwiched between two barges in photograph N43026, below. Originally the lift operated on a hydraulic system, with two counter-balanced water-tight tanks raising and lowering boats, but it was electrified in 1908 and the system modified so that the tanks could be operated independently. The whole system was powered by a tiny 30 horsepower electric motor. In 1983 corrosion of the main support legs forced British Waterways to shut the lift down, but a renovation programme has now returned the lift to full working order.

NORTHWICH, THE ANDERTON BOAT LIFT c1960 N43026

Cheshire's important salt industry has helped develop many other industries based on salt. In 1873 John Brunner and Ludwig Monk purchased the Winnington Hall estate near Northwich, where they established a plant that produced soda ash from salt. In 1926 Brunner Mond merged with other companies to form the chemical giant Imperial Chemical Industries Ltd (ICI). Brine from the salt works is now used to make a range of alkali products for the glass, cosmetic, fabric, paper and pharmaceutical industries.

Salt from Cheshire's saltfields was behind the growth of both Runcorn and Widnes, and many industries dependent on the use of salt had developed in the area by the mid 1800s. It was at this time that Runcorn became a major producer of soap – by 1816 there were already two factories there producing soap and turpentine. A linked industry was the production of alkali, an essential ingredient of soap but also needed in the production of glass and for the finishing of textiles. By the late 19th century the production of alkali was the major industry in the area, but the pollution from the chemical industries here was the worst in Britain. However, in the 21st century all has changed – the air is clean once more, and the Widnes and Runcorn area has become a sought-after place in which to live.

Someone who wanted to live in Runcorn in the early 20th century but never actually got there was Edward John Smith, the captain of the ill-fated 'Titanic'; he bought a retirement home in Higher Runcorn but never moved in, having gone down with his ship when it sank after colliding with an iceberg in 1912.

Runcorn is sited on the south bank of the River Mersey, where the estuary narrows to a point known as the Runcorn Gap. For centuries the Mersey has been an important means of access into the heart of England. In the early 10th century the Anglo-Saxon Queen Ethelfleda, Lady of the Mercians and daughter of Alfred the Great, built a castle at Runcorn to protect her realm from Viking attack. The remains of her castle were discovered when the foundations for the railway bridge were built beside Runcorn in the 1860s, and local people have always called this bridge the Ethelfleda Bridge.

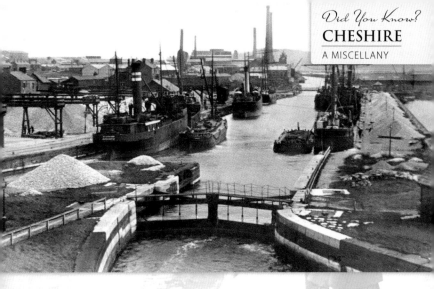

RUNCORN, THE DOCKS c1900 R67301

Runcorn's position on the Mersey meant that it first developed as a small port serving towns further up the river valley. Photograph R67301 (above) shows the docks c1900 at Weston Point, Runcorn. The enormous piles of white stone are heaps of china clay from Cornwall, awaiting trans-shipment onto narrowboats to be taken to the china factories in Stoke-on-Trent. Later the finished article would be exported through here – in 1883 alone, 50,000 tons of china goods were exported through this port.

Accessed off Highlands Road in Runcorn is Runcorn Hill Local Nature Reserve. In the 1800s this area was one vast quarry. Stone from there was used to build the docks at Liverpool and Tatton Hall in nearby Knutsford, and perhaps also the docks in New York, having travelled there as ballast in sailing ships. Runcorn stone was also particularly good for sharpening tools, and was exported for this purpose to tool manufacturers all around the world. By the 1900s the best stone had been worked out from the area, and it was laid out as parkland. It is now an important nature reserve that includes woodland walks as well as north Cheshire's largest surviving stretch of heathland.

The Transporter (more correctly 'transbordeur') Bridge over the Runcorn Gap between Runcorn and Widnes was opened in 1905 (seen on the right of photograph R67043, below). This bridge was a meccano-like structure below which moved a suspension cab, or 'car', carrying vehicles and foot passengers. On the Widnes side of the bridge the world's first double-decker bus service was started in 1909 especially to meet passengers from the bridge and take them into town. The bridge's limited capacity caused problems as traffic increased – in the 1950s car drivers sometimes waited for two hours in the queue. The problem was with the opening of the new Runcorn Bridge in 1961, and this photograph shows the old and new bridges side by side for a brief period before the old Transporter Bridge was demolished. Within 15 years the new bridge needed to be widened, and when this work was completed in 1977 it was renamed the Silver Jubilee Bridge in honour of Queen Elizabeth II's Silver Jubilee that year.

RUNCORN, THE RUNCORN BRIDGE AND THE TRANSPORTER BRIDGE 1961 R67043

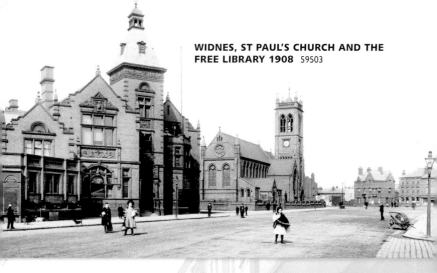

WIDNES, ST PAUL'S CHURCH AND THE FREE LIBRARY 1908 59503

Widnes was formerly in Lancashire but was ceded to Cheshire in 1974. The library in Widnes has one of the largest collections of railway books of any public library in Britain – there are around 6,000 books on the subject. Widnes also has Europe's only museum dedicated solely to the chemical industry – the Catalyst Science and Discovery Centre in Mersey Road, which incorporates part of the former offices and laboratories of what was once Britain's largest soap manufacturing firm, Gossage Soaps, which eventually became part of the Unilever Group.

In 1909 Widnes became the first place in Britain to have a regular covered-top double-decker bus service.

WIDNES, TOWN HALL SQUARE c1965 W97059

Warrington, on the north bank of the Mersey, was also formerly in Lancashire but was ceded to Cheshire in 1974. The town prospered as a centre for a variety of industries in the 18th and 19th centuries, including glass-making, pin production (recalled in the street name of Pinners Brow), clock-making, tanning, sailcloth manufacture, iron and steel works, textile, soap-making and chemical industries, and brewing. By the early 20th century, Warrington could claim to be 'the Town of Many Industries'. Commercial barges glided along the Bridgewater Canal, and ocean-going vessels brought raw materials along the Manchester Ship Canal (see page 44) and exported the products of north-western industries.

Warrington's Town Hall was formerly Bank Hall, built 1749-50 by the famous architect James Gibbs for a local businessman. The ornate Town Hall Gates seen in photograph 36688 (below) were originally designed by the Coalbrookdale Iron Company for Sandringham House in Norfolk; they were adapted by replacing the central Prince of Wales Feathers with the Warrington Coat of Arms. The Town Gates were decorated in their royal colours to celebrate the Silver Jubilee of Queen Elizabeth II in 1977.

A monument in Queen's Gardens in Warrington commemorates the local soldiers of the South Lancashire Regiment who were killed in South Africa during the Boer War. Alfred Drury's bronze statue features Lt Colonel McCarthy O'Leary who was killed in the conflict, and who is also commemorated in the name of O'Leary Street in Warrington.

WARRINGTON, THE TOWN HALL, THE NEW GATES 1895 36688

WARRINGTON, CHURCH STREET 1894 33805

A church at Warrington dedicated to St Elphin is recorded in the Domesday Book of 1086. Much of the present building dates from Victorian reconstruction work commissioned by Rev William Quekett between 1858-62. When the church was restored, its exceptionally high spire was topped with a weathercock gilded with gold coins raised from a fundraising appeal by Rev Quekett with the slogan 'a guinea for a golden cock' – although the money was actually raised in sovereigns, a gold coin worth £1. The original weathercock was replaced about 50 years ago, and was again gilded with sovereigns.

In 1648 a Royalist Scottish army crossed into England and clashed with Oliver Cromwell's forces at Winwick, near Warrington. Following the battle, Cromwell lodged in the town. Photograph 33805 (above) shows the Tudor cottages on the corner of Church Street with Eldon Street which popular tradition associates with Cromwell's visit to Warrington. However, Cromwell did not in fact sleep here, but lodged next door at the Spotted Leopard Inn, later the General Wolfe pub. To commemorate the tercentenary of Oliver Cromwell's birth in 1899, Councillor Frederick Monks presented a statue of Cromwell to the town. It now stands at the side of the Academy building in Bridge Street, home of the Warrington Guardian newspaper.

The Manchester Ship Canal was begun in 1883 and was a major civil engineering project of the Victorian age. When it opened in 1894, the 35.5 mile-long-canal linked new sections of waterway to the River Mersey, enabling ocean-going vessels to reach the new inland port of Manchester and the neighbouring Lancashire cotton towns. The Latchford railway viaduct near Warrington, seen in the background of photograph W29010 (below), was built to carry the London & North Western Railway line from Manchester via Stockport and Warrington to Liverpool. Whilst the Latchford viaduct is high enough to allow the tallest ships to pass beneath, a series of swing bridges allow vessels to pass through most crossings along the canal. In the foreground of this photograph is the Knutsford Road Swing Bridge, which carries the A50 road between Warrington and Knutsford over the canal; the swing bridge rests on 60 rollers operated by hydraulic power to move its 1,350 tons of weight.

WARRINGTON, THE MANCHESTER SHIP CANAL, KNUTSFORD ROAD BRIDGE c1955 W29010

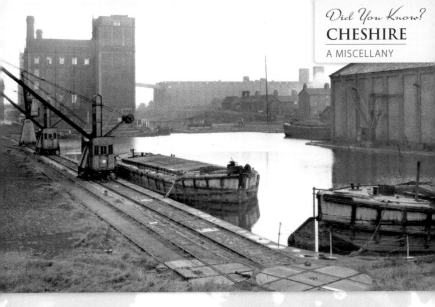

ELLESMERE PORT, FLOUR MILLS AND THE DOCKS c1955 E135009

The opening of the Manchester Ship Canal in 1894 gave countless industries on the Mersey a chance to import and export more cheaply and easily, and was a major factor in the development and prosperity of Ellesmere Port, on the southern border of the Wirral Peninsula north of Chester. Ellesmere Port was created in the 1790s when the Earl of Ellesmere constructed a canal from Ellesmere in Shropshire to meet the River Mersey, to bring goods from the Potteries to Liverpool for world-wide distribution. The canal connected to the Mersey in the village of Netherpool, and the basin where the canal met the river was originally known as Whitby Locks, but was soon renamed Ellesmere Port. Ellesmere Port was a favourite dock for timber from Russia and Scandinavia, which was moved from here all over the north for house building. Photograph E135009 (above) shows a 1950s' view of the docks that linked the Ellesmere Canal (now called the Shropshire Union Canal) with the Manchester Ship Canal, with tall flour mills in the background.

SPORTING CHESHIRE

The Chester Cup horserace, run at the Roodee at Chester in May, is one of the highlights of the horseracing season, formerly known as the St George's Plate because it was run on St George's Day, 23rd April. In the 19th century it was thought to be the country's second biggest betting race after the Epsom Derby.

One of Britain's greatest jockeys was Steve Donoghue, born in Warrington in 1884. He won the Derby six time, a feat nobody else has achieved. He also won eight other 'classics' and was Champion Jockey for ten successive years. Affectionately known as 'Our Steve' by the public, he was extremely popular, and was never called before the stewards after a race.

The Royal Chester Rowing Club has been in existence for over 160 years, and the Chester Regatta is thought to date back to at least 1733. The Rowing Club has produced many fine rowers including, in more recent times, world championship gold medallist Lisa Eyre, and Olympic silver medal winner Richard Stanhope.

Macclesfield was the birthplace of three notable sporting characters of recent times: Jonathan Agnew (born 1960), a successful cricketer with Leicestershire and England, who took 666 first-class wickets and played three times for his country; England football international Peter Crouch (born 1981), famously the tallest man ever to play for the England team; and Britain's most successful Olympic sailor ever, Charles ('Ben') Ainslie (born 1977).

In the 1969/70 season, Macclesfield Town Football Club were the first ever winners of the new national non-League competition, the FA Trophy. They won the trophy at Wembley, in front of a crowd of over 28,000.

In 1882 England played Australia in a cricket match and lost so disastrously that they ceremoniously burned the bails used in the match. Ever since then, Australia and England have played for 'the Ashes' of the bails. The captain of that unfortunate England team in 1882 was Albert Hornby, and he is buried in the churchyard at Acton, near Nantwich.

Crewe's football club, Crewe Alexandra, is the oldest club in the Football League, having been founded in 1876.

Chester was the birthplace of England international footballer Michael Owen, whose father Leslie 'Terry' Owen played for Chester City FC. Chester City FC was formally wound up in 2010 and a new supporter-owned club was formed, Chester FC, which plays its home matches at the Deva Stadium. The stadium is unusual in that most of the ground is actually in Wales, although the main offices and half of the east stand are in England.

The Warrington Wolves Rugby League Club is one of the original rugby clubs that formed the Northern Rugby Football Union in 1895. One of the Wolves' most famous players was Brian Bevan, and there is a statue of him in the town. An Australian, he played for the club for 16 years, from 1945 to 1962. His greatness as a player lay in his try scoring – his career total of 796 is over 200 greater than the second-placed player, Billy Boston, and he scored 3 or more tries in a game more than 100 times. There is a strong rivalry between the Warrington Wolves and the Widnes Vikings RLFC, also one of the original clubs that formed the NRFU. The traditional nickname of the Widnes Vikings is 'The Chemics', a reference to Widnes's chemical industries.

QUIZ QUESTIONS

Answers on page 52.

1. What creature does the old Cheshire dialect word 'bullyed' refer to?

2. What feature of the landscape is known as a 'flash' in Cheshire?

3. When, how and why do the people of Nantwich celebrate 'Holly Holy Day'?

4. What is the Chester Imp, and where can you find it?

5. Who holds the title of Earl of Chester?

6. What was Macclesfield Stripe, and where in the town can you see an example of it?

7. Why was Congleton known as 'Bear Town' in the past?

8. What were known as 'Weaver flats'?

9. In Warrington Museum and Art Gallery is a theatrical object which is unique in Britain – what is it?

10. In which Cheshire town does the custom of 'sanding' take place, and what does this involve?

NANTWICH, THE CHESHIRE CAT c1965 N3036

RECIPE

CHESHIRE CHEESE SOUP

The Cheshire Plain was historically a famous area for cheesemaking, and for many centuries the crumbly, nutty Cheshire Cheese was produced on nearly every farm in the region. The matured cheeses would then have been brought to markets in the local towns, particularly to Nantwich, where an annual cheese fair was established in 1820. Production of this farm-made cheese peaked in 1907, when 600,000 hundredweight was produced locally. Nantwich now holds an International Cheese Show every summer as part of the Nantwich Show, which is the biggest cheese festival in the world. Cheshire Cheese is said to be Britain's oldest cheese, and is mentioned in the Domesday Book of 1086. It was also well-known enough in France to be described in the following rhyme:

> *'Into the Cheshire cheese, dry and pink,*
> *The long teeth of the English sink'.*

> 600ml/1 pint good chicken or vegetable stock
> 275g/10oz potatoes, peeled and finely diced
> 2 leeks, washed, trimmed and chopped
> 2 carrots, peeled and finely chopped or grated
> 25g/1oz oatmeal
> 115g/4oz grated Cheshire Cheese
> Salt and pepper

Put the stock into a large pan, add the vegetables and seasoning and bring to the boil. Simmer for 15 minutes, then add the oatmeal and simmer for a further 10-15 minutes, stirring occasionally, until the vegetables are tender. Just before serving, add half the cheese and stir until melted, then pour the soup into individual serving bowls and sprinkle the remaining cheese on top.

RECIPE

CHESHIRE PARKIN

Parkin is a dark, heavy, sweet, sticky cake made with oatmeal as well as flour. Parkin was traditionally eaten on Bonfire Night (or Guy Fawkes' Night) on 5th November. It is best left in an airtight container before several days before eating, which allows it to develop a good flavour and sticky texture.

> 225g/8oz coarse oatmeal
> 75g/3oz plain flour
> 50g/2oz brown sugar
> 1 teaspoonful ground ginger
> ½ teaspoonful bicarbonate of soda
> A pinch of salt
> 225g/8oz golden syrup or black treacle
> 125g/4oz butter or margarine
> 70ml/2½fl oz milk

Pre-heat the oven to 180°C/350°F/Gas Mark 4.

Mix the dry ingredients together. Melt the syrup or treacle and butter or margarine in a pan and add to the dry ingredients, and stir in the milk to make a soft consistency. Grease a 20cm (7-8 inch) square tin and line it with greaseproof paper. Pour in the mixture, and bake in the middle of the pre-heated oven for about 1¼ hours, when the parkin should be firm to the touch. Leave in the tin to cool completely before cutting into squares, then store in an airtight tin for at least 2 days before eating.

QUIZ ANSWERS

1. 'Bullyed' is an old Cheshire dialect word for a tadpole.

2. A 'flash' is the name given to one of the small lakes in the salt-producing area of Cheshire which are caused by ground subsidence due to salt extraction. The resulting depressions fill with water, creating miniature lakes, many of which have become important wildlife habitats and recreational venues.

3. During the Civil War, the people of Nantwich supported Parliament against Charles I, and Parliamentary forces based their garrison there. Nantwich was besieged by the Royalists for 6 weeks from December until 25th January 1644, when the town was relieved by a force of Parliamentarians in the 'battle of Nantwich'. On the Saturday closest to 25th January each year, known as Holly Holy Day, the local people wear a sprig of holly in their hats to commemorate that victory.

4. The Chester Imp is the name given to a grotesque stone figure in the north clerestory of the nave of Chester Cathedral.

5. The title of the Earl of Chester is conferred on the male heir to the throne of the United Kingdom. It is currently held by Prince Charles.

6. Macclesfield Stripe was a fabric made in the town which was woven with a crepe warp and a spun silk weft. This made the material drape well, but it was also very durable and could be

washed at a high temperature, so it was ideal for making items like handkerchiefs, blouses and dresses. It was very popular in the 1920s and 1930s. The costume collection of the museum at the Heritage Centre holds examples of Macclesfield Stripe.

7. The cruel sport of bear-baiting was so popular in Congleton in Elizabethan times that when the town's bear died just before the annual Wakes, the local people were so anxious to replace it so that the celebrations would not be spoiled that the Congleton Corporation used the money set aside to buy a new Bible for the parish church to buy a new bear instead. The story is recalled in the bear that appears on the town crest, and ever since then the town has been known by the nickname of 'Bear Town'.

8. 'Weaver flats' were flat-bottomed sailing barges used on the River Weaver. They were built locally, with a strong hull so they could sit on the mud at low tide, even with a full cargo on board.

9. In Warrington Museum and Art Gallery is a Roman actor's mask, which was found at Wilderspool. It is the only example found in Britain.

10. Royal May Day in Knutsford includes the tradition of 'sanding' the streets, when the town's pavements are decorated with mottos and patterns made from coloured sand. It is said to derive from the time of King Canute (after whom Knutsford is believed to have been named) who congratulated a newly married local couple, wishing them as many children as the grains of sand he shook from his shoe. At one time sanding was a wedding custom rather than a May Day event.

FRANCIS FRITH

PIONEER VICTORIAN PHOTOGRAPHER

Francis Frith, founder of the world-famous photographic archive, was a complex and multi-talented man. A devout Quaker and a highly successful Victorian businessman, he was philosophical by nature and pioneering in outlook. By 1855 he had already established a wholesale grocery business in Liverpool, and sold it for the astonishing sum of £200,000, which is the equivalent today of over £15,000,000. Now in his thirties, and captivated by the new science of photography, Frith set out on a series of pioneering journeys up the Nile and to the Near East.

INTRIGUE AND EXPLORATION

He was the first photographer to venture beyond the sixth cataract of the Nile. Africa was still the mysterious 'Dark Continent', and Stanley and Livingstone's historic meeting was a decade into the future. The conditions for picture taking confound belief. He laboured for hours in his wicker dark-room in the sweltering heat of the desert, while the volatile chemicals fizzed dangerously in their trays. Back in London he exhibited his photographs and was 'rapturously cheered' by members of the Royal Society. His reputation as a photographer was made overnight.

VENTURE OF A LIFE-TIME

By the 1870s the railways had threaded their way across the country, and Bank Holidays and half-day Saturdays had been made obligatory by Act of Parliament. All of a sudden the working man and his family were able to enjoy days out, take holidays, and see a little more of the world.

With typical business acumen, Francis Frith foresaw that these new tourists would enjoy having souvenirs to commemorate their days out. For the next thirty years he travelled the country by train and by pony and trap, producing fine photographs of seaside resorts and beauty spots that were keenly bought by millions of Victorians. These prints were painstakingly pasted into family albums and pored over during the dark nights of winter, rekindling precious memories of summer excursions. Frith's studio was soon supplying retail shops all over the country, and by 1890 F Frith & Co had become the greatest specialist photographic publishing company in the world, with over 2,000 sales outlets, and pioneered the picture postcard.

FRANCIS FRITH'S LEGACY

Francis Frith had died in 1898 at his villa in Cannes, his great project still growing. By 1970 the archive he created contained over a third of a million pictures showing 7,000 British towns and villages.

Frith's legacy to us today is of immense significance and value, for the magnificent archive of evocative photographs he created provides a unique record of change in the cities, towns and villages throughout Britain over a century and more. Frith and his fellow studio photographers revisited locations many times down the years to update their views, compiling for us an enthralling and colourful pageant of British life and character.

We are fortunate that Frith was dedicated to recording the minutiae of everyday life. For it is this sheer wealth of visual data, the painstaking chronicle of changes in dress, transport, street layouts, buildings, housing and landscape that captivates us so much today, offering us a powerful link with the past and with the lives of our ancestors.

Computers have now made it possible for Frith's many thousands of images to be accessed almost instantly. The archive offers every one of us an opportunity to examine the places where we and our families have lived and worked down the years. Its images, depicting our shared past, are now bringing pleasure and enlightenment to millions around the world a century and more after his death.

For further information visit: www.francisfrith.com

INTERIOR DECORATION

Frith's photographs can be seen framed and as giant wall murals in thousands of pubs, restaurants, hotels, banks, retail stores and other public buildings throughout Britain. These provide interesting and attractive décor, generating strong local interest and acting as a powerful reminder of gentler days in our increasingly busy and frenetic world.

FRITH PRODUCTS

All Frith photographs are available as prints and posters in a variety of different sizes and styles. In the UK we also offer a range of other gift and stationery products illustrated with Frith photographs, although many of these are not available for delivery outside the UK – see our web site for more information on the products available for delivery in your country.

THE INTERNET

Over 100,000 photographs of Britain can be viewed and purchased on the Frith web site. The web site also includes memories and reminiscences contributed by our customers, who have personal knowledge of localities and of the people and properties depicted in Frith photographs. If you wish to learn more about a specific town or village you may find these reminiscences fascinating to browse. Why not add your own comments if you think they would be of interest to others? See **www.francisfrith.com**

PLEASE HELP US BRING FRITH'S PHOTOGRAPHS TO LIFE

Our authors do their best to recount the history of the places they write about. They give insights into how particular towns and villages developed, they describe the architecture of streets and buildings, and they discuss the lives of famous people who lived there. But however knowledgeable our authors are, the story they tell is necessarily incomplete.

Frith's photographs are so much more than plain historical documents. They are living proofs of the flow of human life down the generations. They show real people at real moments in history; and each of those people is the son or daughter of someone, the brother or sister, aunt or uncle, grandfather or grandmother of someone else. All of them lived, worked and played in the streets depicted in Frith's photographs.

We would be grateful if you would give us your insights into the places shown in our photographs: the streets and buildings, the shops, businesses and industries. Post your memories of life in those streets on the Frith website: what it was like growing up there, who ran the local shop and what shopping was like years ago; if your workplace is shown tell us about your working day and what the building is used for now. Read other visitors' memories and reconnect with your shared local history and heritage. With your help more and more Frith photographs can be brought to life, and vital memories preserved for posterity, and for the benefit of historians in the future.

Wherever possible, we will try to include some of your comments in future editions of our books. Moreover, if you spot errors in dates, titles or other facts, please let us know, because our archive records are not always completely accurate—they rely on 140 years of human endeavour and hand-compiled records. You can email us using the contact form on the website.

Thank you!

For further information, trade, or author enquiries please contact us at the address below:

The Francis Frith Collection, Oakley Business Park, Wylye Road, Dinton, Wiltshire SP3 5EU.
Tel: +44 (0)1722 716 376 Fax: +44 (0)1722 716 881
e-mail: sales@francisfrith.co.uk **www.francisfrith.com**